The Passion of Christ

The
Passion
of
Christ

a discourse by

Swami Shri Kripalvanandji

Kripalu Publications, Box 120, Summit Station, PA 17979

Library of Congress Catalog Card Number: 83-80214
ISBN: 0-940258-09-9

Printed in the United States of America
by Kripalu Publications
P.O. Box 120
Summit Station, PA 17979

Contents

Swami Kripalvanandji (left) and Yogi Amrit Desai

Foreword

Yogi Amrit Desai, one of Swami Shri Kripalvanandji's closest disciples, painted the crucifixion of Christ that is seen on the cover of this book and authored the ensuing foreword. It is fitting that he introduce this book. Swami Kripalvanandji, recognizing the West's spiritual thirst for the true teachings of yoga, delegated Yogi Amrit Desai to teach in this country. Yogi Desai developed Kripalu Yoga, founded the Kripalu Center for Holistic Health, Kripalu Yoga Ashram and Kripalu Yoga Retreat, all of which he named after his gurudev. When Swami Kripalvanandji first arrived in this country, he was already well-known and loved through the service of his disciple.

Swami Shri Kripalvanandji (whom I affectionately call Bapuji) was always interested in the teachings of Christ. When he accepted my invitation to come to this country, he studied the teachings of Christ in greater depth in order to truly understand the spiritual and religious background of many of the people he would meet in the West.

Bapuji had copies of the Bible that were written in Gujarati, his native language. He also obtained copies in English, one of which was richly illustrated with reproductions of paintings by well-known artists. One of the paintings of the crucifixion of Christ touched Bapuji very deeply. Whenever he looked at that reproduction, seeing what sometimes happens to those who follow the path of truth and love, his eyes would fill with tears.

The profound stirring that Bapuji felt in his heart for Christ is evident throughout this discourse. Bapuji was a spiritual master who lived a life of pure love and dedication to humanity. Because of his own experience in trying to bring love and truth to the world, Bapuji felt love for Christ; and he could also understand the manner in which people often treat truth and truth's messenger.

Bapuji recognized that the life of Christ embodied truth. Bapuji could relate to the truth so readily that he never considered Christ's life to be foreign or to be an event that happened in the past. Whenever he reflected upon Christ, Bapuji would move beyond time and space and become so attuned to the life of Christ that it became a living reality for him, and it touched his heart deeply.

Bapuji believed that Christ was an enlightened master, one who realized that the problems in people's lives emerged from the lies they lived. In Christ's time the traditional way of deciding what constituted right conduct had been strongly influenced by the cultural and social applications of religion, rather than the true purpose of religion. When Christ saw that people suffered because they had adapted their religion to the dictates of society and culture rather than to the truth, he could not tolerate it. He wanted to help people, but he could only help them by bringing them the truth — regardless of the consequences he had to suffer in order to do that.

Bapuji saw that Christ's mission was to alleviate people's suffering by helping them rise above society's idea of religion and live according to the truth. That is what Christ demonstrated in his life. Bapuji felt that even in this day and age, in order to receive the full benefit of Christ's teachings, we must rise above the current traditions and cultural aspects of Christian religion and go to the heart, the essence of the teachings of Christ; then only can Christ come alive.

Bapuji's message for us is this: if we want true freedom and spiritual awakening, we must be willing to bear the cross, to experience the trials that truth will put us through before it will make us free. We must be willing to carry our own crosses in order to experience the Christ within ourselves and to follow the path of truth and love.

25 *December 1980*
Thursday, A.M.
Kripalu Yoga Ashram
Sumneytown, Pa.

Introduction

I have concentrated only on the events in the life of Christ which have touched my heart most deeply.

In my preparation I consulted mainly Matthew's Gospel, and occasionally I referred to Luke's Gospel. In some instances, I have followed strictly the texts of the Gospels; in some instances, I have reworded the texts while retaining the original meaning; in other cases, I have embellished the authors' texts. In still other instances, I have allowed my imagination free reign within the bounds of general psychological principles.

I have also examined many pictures of Christ in books depicting events in his life. This includes the picture book *Jesus of Nazareth,* which was published by the producers of the film of the same name. I have been inspired by many photographs depicting the events leading to Christ's crucifixion such as the picture of Christ being whipped; the one in which he is being mocked and is wearing a crown of thorns; the picture in which he is forced to carry his own cross; and the picture of Christ on the cross. Another book I have examined depicted Christ being crucified. This book by a famous artist contains excellent reproductions of paintings which were extremely heart-rending. The reader is requested to read this story while keeping the above-mentioned facts in mind.

The Author

Chapter 1

The Revelation of the Crucifixion

The atmosphere was still. Lord Christ's twelve disciples sat around him.

Observing their guru* engrossed in deep thought and knowing that whatever he would say would be worth listening to, all of them waited silently.

Lifting his eyes from his point of concentration, Lord Christ looked around at the eager faces of his disciples.

He spoke softly. "Now only two days remain before the Passover arrives. After it is over, the authorities will arrest me and crucify me." His words revealed his pure vision without a trace of fear or depression.

Not one of the disciples was surprised by this revelation. After observing the current situation, it was obvious to everyone that such an event would soon come to pass.

Until he was an adolescent, Lord Christ had lived with his family. The events of his life from the ages of twelve to thirty are a mystery. When he emerged from seclusion and returned to society at the age of thirty, the entire society was profoundly influenced by his personality. During the next three years he continually spread religion.

*guru — spiritual master who guides the disciple across the darkness of ignorance to the light of knowledge (gu=darkness; ru=light)

During that period, the twelve close disciples of Christ were profoundly influenced by their guru's thought, speech, and conduct. Moreover, whenever people heard of Lord Christ's appearance in their area, they would flock to his side from wherever they were. Lord Christ's disciples greatly loved their guru's fame, for they too received the same respect everywhere. Therefore, their enthusiasm increased day by day.

As Lord Christ's fame increased, so did the concern of his enemies. They began to criticize Lord Christ and spread rumors among the people: "This Jesus is not the Son of God. He believes himself to be God's messenger; he constantly blasphemes the sacred scriptures and claims to speak the word of God. But his words, in reality, are not the words of God. Of course, some may give him recognition as a poet or an orator; but, even among them, his status can only be at the bottom. We consider him to be a fraud. Yes, he is eloquent. That is why all of you are swayed by his oratory. But he does not have any power to cure the diseased. So what if from among thousands of people twenty or twenty-five are cured and a few more show some improvement in their condition? There is no miracle in this. Neither is there any truth in Jesus' claims about raising the dead.

"Events that occur in this world which appear to be miracles are, in fact, miracles; they are not the work of a human being. Only God Himself has the power to manifest miracles. Lowly human beings do not have such power. Of course, man can become an instrument in such cases. But, deceitful men like Jesus usually claim: 'If you keep unshakeable faith in me, you will be cured of your disease. Not only that, but you will be able to witness your dead relatives restored to life.'

"This false statement can be refuted with simple logic. If faith is essential in manifesting miracles, then the miracle which manifests is not the miracle of the person claiming to perform it. It is, instead, the miracle of the person who has faith. Pure and unshakeable faith is divine energy which has the full capacity to manifest miracles. Saints consider such faith to be the grace of God. When a traveler sits in a vehicle, it does not move on the strength of the traveler's faith. The vehicle moves on its own strength. Likewise, accomplished masters do not need anyone's faith. They can create extraordinary miracles with the power of their own accomplishments. Jesus' miracles do not have the strength of his accomplishments. They are merely the result of people's imaginations.

"Do not believe, however, that we are atheists. We are theists as you are, but our faith is not as blind as yours. We not only seek truth, we worship it. Yet, we are extremely cautious. We have asked Jesus to heal diseases in our presence. We have said to him: 'We will collect one hundred patients; and if you will cure only ten of them, in the time limit decided by you, we will gladly acknowledge your greatness with due respect.'

"Jesus also claims that he raises the dead. We have told him: 'We will collect only ten dead people; and if you will raise just three of them, we will not only become your lifelong followers, but we will assist you wholeheartedly in spreading the news.' But he has not responded to our request. Thus we are more strongly convinced that there is nothing but hypocrisy in his propagation. Do not think we have not investigated him objectively. We have, in fact, investigated honestly. Yet, we have not found any genuineness in him."

The campaign of Christ's adversaries became stronger and stronger each day. As a result, the same subject was discussed throughout the land. Even the minds of Lord Christ's closest disciples were bewildered and fearful. They felt that, because there were many powerful people among Christ's opponents, the opposition would ultimately cause trouble. Lord Christ's enemies were determined to accomplish their aim to defeat him.

Faith which stands solely on the foundation of logic

collapses to the ground as soon as logic becomes unsteady. Such faith cannot be called true faith.

True faith is like the grace of God. No unfavorable circumstances can shake it in the least.

If the disciples had heard these words: "The adversaries will arrest me to crucify me," from the mouth of their own guru, it is possible that they may have inferred that the guru might have been frightened also. But it is worth noting that the average person is unable to imagine the willpower of the great masters. In fact, one can never imagine it. The words uttered by such great men are preserved intact for thousands of years. Although their words seem common, they are extraordinary. They contain more than the energy of thought; they carry the energy of conduct. The collective strength of thought and conduct is called the "strength of *tapas*." Such words are called "the energy of the soul," "divine energy," "God's will," or "the Word of God." Great teachers have the capacity to influence large masses of people. Therefore, even if everyone in the world were to oppose them, they would never be shaken.

It was time to leave. All thirteen of them rose together and began walking slowly toward their destination. Their lips were sealed; only the sound of their walking clattered against their eardrums.

Chapter 2

The Plot Against Lord Christ

Today the assembly of Christ's enemies had gathered in the palace of Caiaphas, the high priest. The courtyard was huge. Elaborate arrangements had been made to welcome the participants. Many elders had come to participate in the assembly. It was indeed an important meeting; therefore, precautions had been taken to insure that no uninvited guests were present. Silence pervaded the area.

The proceedings began.

An eminent high priest stood up and convened the assembly with a brief introduction. "In the beginning, we did not pay much attention to the wanton acts of Jesus. Later, however, we realized that if we weren't careful, he would draw innocent people onto the wrong path.

"The scriptures describe the concept of duality between the Lord and the devotee, and we have had faith in this concept for hundreds of years. Yet, the principles that Jesus has been spreading recently differ greatly from our sacred scriptures. Apparently, he has imported these new principles here from some other country. His teachings espouse the concept of non-duality. He claims: 'I and my Father are one.' But how can the father-son relationship be expressed in the concept of non-duality? Jesus appears to propound the concepts of both duality and non-duality.

"A devotee cannot be called God. He can never be God.

Yes, he does have a ray of the Lord's light, so he is not different from God. But God is an ocean, and the devotee is a drop. They are not equal under any circumstances.

"In one instance Jesus claims that he is the representative of God; in another he claims that he is a prophet of God; then he claims that he himself is God. There is no end to the extent of his ego. It is our opinion that it is not God who has descended into him, but Satan. Doubtless, Satan will never be persuaded by any of our holy teachings. Thus, we should give up all our attempts to convince him of his error. Instead, we should arrest him and condemn him to death."

Other speakers, in turn, also described Christ's errors in great detail. Eventually, they expressed their verdict: that he must be put to death.

One speaker recounted, "When some of the high priests approached Jesus for advice in the judgment of the adulteress, he favored the side of debauchery rather than chastity. His underlying meaning was this: 'Since every person practices debauchery overtly or covertly, this woman deserves forgiveness.' But Jesus is not aware that proper administration of the law is required for the family, society, and nation to function properly. The administration must allow room for reward, condemnation, and punishment as well."

Finally, the assembly discussed how Christ should be killed.

The elders advised against hastily putting him to death. They decided that to avoid being held responsible for Christ's death, the best solution was to put him to death through the agency of the state. Besides, if he were put to death during the holy days which were quickly approaching, the people would riot and would severely disrupt the lives of everyone who had a part in this. Taking all these factors into consideration, they concluded: "We should find a way to accomplish our aim so that Jesus is condemned as a traitor and we do not appear to be involved in it at all."

Chapter 3

Betrayal of the Guru

To betray the guru is to betray God, religion, scriptures, and one's own Self.

In the same manner that ticks can cling to a cow's udder, yet merely suck its blood instead of drinking its milk, an evil person can live closely with a great teacher as a disciple and be unaffected by their relationship. Even after several years, the false disciple is not able to recognize a single virtue in the guru. Thus, how can such a disciple possibly practice any virtue in his own life?

Only a person who has a particular virtue himself can appreciate that virtue in another person. If one has no virtues, how can he possibly appreciate a saint or a Sadguru* who is a treasure house of virtues?

Judas Iscariot was one of the twelve disciples of Lord Christ. He understood how strongly determined Christ's enemies were, and he realized that his guru would not be able to escape from their net. Judas intended to separate eventually from Lord Christ because he realized that if he didn't, he would regret it in the future. He knew that Lord Christ's enemies would consider the twelve disciples to be dangerous, and that their lives, too, would be in danger.

*Sadguru—a true spiritual master; the highest guru (the prefix *sad* stands for genuineness and trueness of the *guru*)

After finding out who the chief priest was and where he lived, Judas approached him.

One whose feet do not shake while committing the greatest sin, whose heart does not grieve, and who even forgets his humanity, is indeed a great sinner. What possible relationship could he have with religion, guru, God, or scripture?

After bowing down, Judas sat facing the chief priest.

"Who are you?" the chief priest inquired. "Where do you come from and why have you come to see me? I don't know you."

"I have come as your friend with a sincere desire that you accept me as your friend. I am one of the twelve disciples of Jesus. My name is Judas Iscariot."

The priest was exultant. Pretending to be unaffected, however, he lovingly replied, "Welcome my friend. Rest for a few hours while I call some of the leading authorities here. It would be inappropriate for me to talk with you alone."

Several hours passed.

The authorities arrived. After talking with them privately, the chief priest called Judas Iscariot.

They expressed their opinion. "Having seen your good intentions toward us, we accept you as a friend. Now, how can you help us?"

"I will deliver Jesus to you."

"Yes, we have already accepted this as our religious mission; so, at all costs, we will arrest him. However, if you can aid our efforts, we will gladly accept your help."

Judas revealed his selfishness as he interrogated them. "What will you give me as a reward for this task?"

After discussing it among themselves, the authorities replied, "We will give you thirty pieces of silver."

Judas accepted their terms and was immediately given thirty pieces of silver.

Then, the chief priest became serious and said, "Now we would like to ask a few questions. Our intentions are friendly, of course, for we are convinced that you are our friend. Therefore, we have faith that you will answer our questions truthfully."

Judas gave his consent.

"You are one of the twelve closest disciples of Jesus. In a crisis like this, it is your duty to stand beside him. Why have you sided with us instead? Are you afraid of our side?"

"I have sided with you because I am convinced that you are on the side of truth. I am not afraid of your side, but I don't want to invite undue trouble."

"This would mean that our allegations against Jesus are not merely allegations; they are facts."

"Yes, I have contemplated them, and it appears to me that they are true," Judas replied respectfully.

One of the authorities asked, "We have heard that Jesus cures the diseased. How correct is this claim?"

"It is correct to some extent. A few cures have occurred in patients who have strong faith. When Jesus speaks, he speaks with conviction. As a result, his statements become a source of inspiration in the hearts of faithful audiences. Scholars consider him to be merely eloquent, but they too are present in the crowds surrounding him. Their aim, however, is to evaluate his words."

Another authority raised two more questions. "Until now, how many dead people has Jesus raised? And in how many instances were you present?"

"It is widely believed among those who have faith in Jesus that he has raised some persons from the dead. It is difficult, though, to confirm the actual number. It is possible that in some of these cases the person was not really dead, but merely appeared to be dead and was mistakenly declared so. Later, the person may have shown signs of life — signs which then were considered to be the miracles of Jesus. I barely remember whether or not I was present at such events. Moreover, I am an intellectual, and I cannot possibly accept such an event as a miracle unless I experience it directly."

The high priest was pleased with Judas' answers. He repeatedly thanked Judas Iscariot saying, "We are fully satisfied with your answers."

A third authority who, until now, had been quietly listening to the question and answer session gazed intently into the face of Judas Iscariot and said, "Dear friend, if you will permit me, I would also like to ask you one or two questions."

Judas nodded in consent.

"Since you are a disciple of Jesus and have lived close to him, I will consider your answers to be truthful and I will try to contemplate them deeply. Jesus not only considers himself to be a prophet of high caliber, but he persistently tries to convince society of this. And since he utters prophecies from time to time, you must have had the benefit of hearing them. We have heard that people experience some of his prophecies almost immediately. Some people experience other prophecies after several months or after a few years.

"If his prophecies are genuine, surely you too must have been influenced by them. Yet it does not seem so, because if you had been influenced, you would never have joined us. Thus, we have become totally convinced that Jesus' prophecies are inspired by ego rather than by God. Moreover, we have heard that his entire life has been filled with miracles. And, yet, it does not seem that those miracles have influenced your mind. Are my inferences correct?"

"Yes. I am an intellectual; I am not faith-oriented."

Satisfied with that answer, the official continued his probing. "Now, I will ask you a second question. I believe that you are an intellectual. Since you are a disciple, Jesus must have taught you how to eliminate diseases and death. Can you tell us something about those principles? Medicine also alleviates disease and helps resist death to a certain extent. What principles has Jesus taught you about curing diseases through firm faith?"

"Jesus has not taught any principles specifically for that

purpose. From his countless experiments, however, we feel that purity, loving conduct, faith in God, and strong will-power are the major contributing factors. In fact, we have always considered his conduct to be faultless and have, accordingly, been guided by it."

The official fired several other questions at Judas. "Have you ever cured anyone's disease yourself? Have you ever raised anyone from the dead? Do you believe you can do so?"

Judas broke into laughter, and said, "Of course I have carried on many experiments while imitating Jesus, but I have never cured anyone's disease. Not only that, but I have not been able to cure my own diseases. I do remember that whenever some patients confessed to me that their diseases were alleviated, I would reflect deeply upon how this could have happened. But, I have always considered such cases to be mere accidents. I have not raised anyone from the dead. My conscience, in fact, tells me that death and disease cannot be eliminated in ordinary circumstances. Of course, if one has acquired the prestige Jesus has, he would invariably receive credit for the results of other people's faith."

When Judas Iscariot departed, there was swiftness in his legs and boundless enthusiasm in his mind. Just as elephants have teeth both for eating and decoration, a person can be skilled in various types of behavior. What is in one's thoughts may be missing from his speech; and what is in one's speech may be absent from his conduct. This is called malice, or irreligion. Even though an irreligious person may rise to the status of a teacher of religion, he can never spread genuine religion.

Chapter 4

The Last Supper

Today was the first day of Passover. Lord Christ's disciples came to him and asked, "Where do you want us to celebrate the Passover supper?"

He sat with his eyes closed for a moment and then instructed them: "Go to a certain man in the city and give him this message: 'My hour has come. My twelve disciples and I will celebrate the Passover at your house.' "

After his disciples made the arrangements he had requested, Lord Christ went there.

As the supper was about to begin, Lord Christ sat engrossed in observing the setting sun. His contemplation was interrupted by a disciple who came to inform him, "The supper is ready. The time has come to eat. Everyone is waiting for you."

Slowly, Christ followed the disciple.

The meal began.

One disciple, observing his guru's contemplative mood, remarked, "You seem to be deep in thought."

Lord Christ nodded silently in agreement and said, "Although one should not utter any grievous statements during meals, I have a sad statement to make now, for I am helpless in the matter. One of you has joined my adversaries and will hand me over to them."

After hearing this, everyone's faces became distressed.

Close disciples are the very heart of the guru. Disciples close to the guru who have not been influenced by his thought, speech, and conduct can never experience genuine closeness. There are two possible reasons for this: the guru's polluted character or the disciple's polluted character. Genuine intimacy arises only if there is purity in the characters of both guru and disciple. The ordinary relationship is usually superficial. Genuine intimacy must demonstrate complete union of thoughts. Just as a ripe abscess in the body inflicts excruciating pain, a person with a perverted mind inflicts excruciating pain upon his relatives or loved ones.

In critical situations, close disciples should become an impenetrable fortress for the guru and serve him like devoted soldiers. They should not torture him by becoming his enemies.

After hearing Lord Christ's statement, all the disciples began asking the same question, one after the other: "Lord, am I the one who is going to commit this evil deed?"

Lord Christ answered, "The one who dips his hand in the dish with me will betray me."

Everyone's eyes were lowered to the dish.

Judas' hand was in the dish.

With this clarification, the remaining eleven disciples were relieved that they were not moving in the direction of offense. Denying the allegation, Judas spoke. "Master, I am not betraying you. However, given the present circumstances, it is natural for you to believe I am. I am not offended."

To commit a crime is a sin; to hide it or to deny it is a greater sin.

Lord Christ had no desire to debate or to preach; yet, revealing his thoughts, he replied, "By such deeds the lamp of humanity is extinguished. One who has lost his humanity has wasted his life."

Beseeching God for His blessings, Lord Christ tore bread into small pieces. Giving it to his disciples, he said, "Take this and eat. This symbolizes God's blessings. Consider it to be my body."

Then he took a cup, gave thanks to God, asked for His blessings, and instructed everyone. "This is also the blessings of God. Drink it all of you. It is divine nectar. Consider it to be my blood which seals God's covenant—my blood poured out for many for the forgiveness of sins." He further said, "I tell you, I will never again drink this wine until the day I drink new wine in my Father's kingdom."

At the end of the supper, they sang a hymn and then went out to the Mount of Olives.

Chapter 5

The Arrest

Gradually the darkness increased, and night fell.

Christ instructed all of the disciples present. "This very night, all of you will run away and leave me; for the scriptures say: 'God will kill the shepherd, and the sheep of the flock will be scattered.' But after I am raised to life, I will go to Galilee ahead of you."

One of the disciples, whose name was Peter, objected. "No my master, I say this with faith, that in spite of your prediction, this disciple of yours will never leave you today."

Lord Christ smiled as he refuted Peter's statement. "Listen, Peter, I am telling you the truth. It is night now; only a few hours remain until dawn. Remember, before the rooster crows tonight, you will say three times that you do not know me."

Peter was adamant. Elaborating upon the same statement, he said, "My Lord, don't be unjust. I say this with firm determination that even if I have to give up my life, I will do so gladly, but I will never deny you under any circumstances."

Lord Christ remained silent; it was no use arguing. He was well aware that a person's mind changes according to the changing situation.

When they arrived at a place called Gethsemene, Christ

instructed his disciples, "Remain here. I must go to a secluded spot to pray. Peter and the two sons of Zebedee may accompany me."

After walking for awhile, Christ expressed his mental anguish and grief. "Peter, my sorrow is deep, and my soul is greatly distressed. Now my spirit has no desire to remain in my body. Stay here and keep watch with me. I am going to pray."

He went on a little further. Suddenly, he collapsed face downward on the ground. Then, sitting up and bowing his head, he prayed, "Beloved Lord, I am distressed. I am not even able to pray to You with a steady mind. I am not in the least concerned with fame or infamy, praise or criticism, victory or defeat, or life or death. Praying to You is my life; the absence of prayer is death. You are omniscient; You are my protector and my benefactor. Not because I desire it, but only if You wish, take this cup of suffering from me."

This was his silent prayer imbued with his deep feelings of pure devotion.

Such intense feeling is acute concentration, or meditation. When one is engrossed in such a self-inspired meditation, he is not aware of any limitation of time.

Lord Christ could not determine how much time he had spent praying. When he got up and returned to where Peter was sitting, he found Peter asleep. Deeply grieved, he awakened Peter and gently scolded him. "You are a disciple; could you not keep watch with me for one hour?"

Peter was embarrassed. However, embarrassment is not repentence. One who forgets a vow taken even for a few moments is indeed not a sadhak*. A sadhak always remains vigilant. The ability to abide by one's vows indicates one's character.

Lord Christ sat for awhile. His mind was greatly agitated by tumultuous thoughts caused by the disturbing situation. Not wanting to sit there in that state of mind, he again

*sadhak—a spiritual aspirant; a practitioner of yoga

got up to pray. While leaving, he again instructed Peter, "Keep watch and pray constantly. It does not matter if the mind is weak; if your spirit is willing, its strength will definitely permeate your weak mind."

While he was walking, a thought crossed Christ's mind. "What's the use of offering the same prayers again and again? The all-pervading omniscient God knows what the prayer will be long before the devotee utters it. God's plans are all predetermined, and there is no scope for any change. If one is aware of this fact, isn't it disrespectful of God's plans to beseech Him for a change?"

The answer to Lord Christ's questions came to his mind. "In spite of knowing the truth, if one experiences a strong urge to pray, that urge must represent another side of God's plan. Thus, even if the other side seems inappropriate or seems certain to fail, it is proper to accept it as one's own desire and follow it."

He drove the disturbing thoughts from his mind and began praying. "Compassionate Lord, even without my asking, You have always given me everything I need. I have never felt the need to beseech You, for You have never been lacking in generosity. If I beseech You shamelessly now, it is not because I lack faith, but because I have absolute faith. Oh, My Lord, earlier it was easy for me to remain engrossed in thoughts of You. But this ability has left me as a result of this disturbance. It is as if Your very sacred memory has abandoned my mind. Oh, Father of the Universe, it is only for this reason that I have been offering You the same prayer again and again. You are an ocean of compassion. If it is possible, please relieve me of this distress. Life without remembering You appears to me as death." No sooner had his prayer ended than the distressing thoughts again took command of his mind. With a sorrowful heart, he slowly walked to where he had left Peter and the others sitting.

He saw that all of them were sleeping; no one was praying. His sorrow was deepened by their lack of support.

The strength of saints is not based on their accomplishments. It is based on God Himself. God is their everything. Even when all their unfavorable circumstances are converted into favorable ones, their faith, patience, courage, tolerance, and other virtues still must be severely tested. Without such ordeals, the assumption or manifestation of total purity is impossible.

Saint means "a burning lamp." A saint must burn continually. Society will receive light only if he burns. Only then can society be led on a pilgrimage on the path of duty.

Lord Christ called loudly two or three times, "Peter!"

Peter woke up from a deep sleep, rubbed his eyes, and looked up at Lord Christ who was standing close to him. Recollecting some of the events which had happened only a few hours before, Peter confessed with sheer embarrassment, "Master, I am telling you the truth. I tried my best to keep awake and pray according to your advice, but I don't know at what moment I fell asleep. Please forgive me."

"Dear brother, it is better to ask for punishment rather than forgiveness. However, pardoning and punishing are within God's jurisdiction. I sincerely wish that you will receive divine inspiration."

Lord Christ sat there for awhile, then got up for a third time to go pray. While leaving, he again repeated the same advice, "Remain awake and continue praying diligently."

Saints are not violent like swords; they are nonviolent like shields. They have the capacity to endure countless blows. The valor of a shield is extraordinary. It is not afraid in the least while facing the sharp blade of a flashing sword. On the contrary, it not only advances zealously to welcome the sword, it tolerates easily the cruel blows on its body. Saints and shields are both tolerant to the same extent. In fact, it is difficult to judge which of the two is more worthy of admiration, even though a saint is alive, and a shield is inert.

As Lord Christ knelt to pray, his entire being participated in the act. His devotion began to speak: "Beloved Lord, now each moment seems like an age; now this mental distress is more than I can bear. I fear that You have forsaken me, and I feel very lonely and helpless. Everywhere I see only darkness; nowhere do I find a ray of light. A situation has arisen which afflicts me greatly. Oh, Compassionate One, kindly relieve me of this critical situation."

When he returned after praying, Peter was sleeping. Not the least offended, Lord Christ awakened him. Peter was extremely embarrassed as he got up. Lord Christ said sweetly, "Peter, now your sleeping or your keeping awake can no longer matter. Look, the hour is approaching."

No sooner had he uttered those words, than Judas approached him accompanied by a large crowd. This crowd was sent by the high priests and the elders. Many in the crowd were armed with swords; others had clubs in their hands.

Judas had informed the crowd earlier, "The man whose feet I kiss is Jesus; arrest him." He approached Lord Christ and said, "My Lord, shalom." Then, bowing down, he kissed Christ's feet.

Who can possibly believe a disciple to be a close one when he behaves so despicably toward the Sadguru? How can he be called a human being, when, even after three years of continual closeness, his mind is not purified, and he is not affected by the pure conduct, self-control, and saintliness of the virtuous Sadguru?

After Judas' ritual of bowing down was finished, Lord Christ said, "Friend, what is the use of this hypocritical behavior? Do what you have come to do."

And immediately, the crowd arrested Lord Christ.

One of those who was with Lord Christ drew his sword and struck the high priest's slave, cutting off his ear.

Lord Christ saw this. Looking at him, he said, "Dear friend, put your sword back in its place. Remember one thing: all who live by the sword will die by the sword. If I were to call on my Father for help, He would at once send a huge army of angels. But if I had done that, I would have

22 violated the scriptures."

Then, Lord Christ spoke to the crowd. "Friends, I am a man of peace. Did you have to come with swords and clubs to capture me as though I were an outlaw? Every day I sat and taught in the Temple, and you did not arrest me. But all this has happened in order to bring to pass what the prophets have spoken in the scriptures."

By the time he had finished this statement, none of his twelve closest disciples were present. All of them had fled.

To abandon the Sadguru is to abandon religion, God, truth, love, and self-control. One seeks refuge in the Sadguru to acquire knowledge. If one abandons the Sadguru before acquiring knowledge, that abandonment is the abandonment of knowledge itself. In such a desertion, religion, God, truth, love, and self-control are also abandoned. It is the disciple who suffers a loss if he deserts the Sadguru; the guru does not suffer any loss. Such disciples cannot be called genuine or close disciples.

Chapter 6

Utter Disrespect

Only sincere people can protect religion. Non-religious or hypocritically religious people can never do so. Among those who are religious, many are well-versed in the scriptures, but they do not practice religion. Thus, they are not truly religious. Among those who are religious, some are faith-oriented. They do not know scriptures well, but they practice ordinary religion to the best of their capacity. They also, however, are not truly religious. Truly religious people not only know scriptures, but they sincerely practice the virtuous conduct prescribed by the scriptures.

By keenly observing society, one realizes that usually only non-religious or hypocritically religious people are eager to protect religion, and they themselves have been the source of all the troubles. Religion is never protected through them. In fact, their activities offend religion. Religion has never been protected by non-religion.

When any person or society protects religion, it becomes tranquil and trouble-free. Wherever restraint, peace, love, and dedication are lacking, protection of religion is not possible. Those who seek refuge in wantonness, violence, hatred, and selfishness do not protect religion; they manifest the lack of religion inherent in themselves. Their so-called growth is not evolution. It is deterioration or regression.

Well in advance of the event, Lord Christ's enemies received the news that he was to be arrested. A huge crowd of teachers of the Law, elders, and other respected citizens began to gather in the courtyard of Caiaphus, the high priest. Leaders were jubilantly welcoming the visitors. Their fickle minds danced with joy at what they considered their victory and Christ's defeat.

After some time, Lord Christ was escorted into the courtyard in the company of the crowd which had gone to witness his arrest.

Many among them were seeing Lord Christ for the first time. His young age of thirty-three, his radiant face, his slender, pure body covered with a long robe, and his confident gait all conspired to reveal his charismatic personality.

Peter also had come secretly to find out what was going on. In order to see and hear everything without being spotted by anyone he knew, he concealed himself.

This was a religious assembly in name only. It did not have to make a decision on behalf of religion or irreligion, for the decision to crucify Lord Christ had been made long before this jury was convened. Their hatred itself was judgment. This assembly was giving irreligion the appearance of religion. Not only that, but in order to accomplish its purpose, the jury had gathered false evidence and witnesses. In spite of this, they had not achieved the expected result.

Eventually, two false witnesses were found. They stated, "We have heard Jesus say 'I am going to tear down God's temple and build it again in three days.' "

The high priest stood up and asked Lord Christ, "Did you speak those words? These witnesses are giving evidence against you. Why are you standing there silently? Why don't you answer?"

Lord Christ stood there in silence.

Again the high priest spoke to him. "In the name of the living God, I now put you under oath. Tell us if you are the Messiah, the Son of God."

A person of blind intellect would never be able to discern the correct answer to such a question. Even if he were given the correct answer, he would never accept it. Only a person of faith would know the answer without the question even being asked.

Christ was, in fact, the Son of God. Every human being is a son of God, but few realize this fact. And even when the realization dawns, most of them forget it in the next moment. Christ never forgot, even for a moment, that he was the Son of God. This was the source of his uniqueness. When one has such a strong realization, how can it be denied that he is a Son of God?

In society, every person expresses the thoughts that he thinks are appropriate, and he has every right to do so. But to accept or reject those thoughts is the privilege of the listener. The listener may or may not accept the speaker's thoughts, but the speaker is not responsible for that fact. The speaker should not even be considered important in this matter. The listener's faith is the important factor.

Christ admitted to being the Son of God, but that was not really his offense. His independent thinking was the offense. Also, it is inappropriate to think that society was led astray as a result of his utterances. Society was continually influenced by some of the aspects of his pure character. If the council considered his declaration inappropriate, it should have appointed another genuine preacher to counteract his influence.

Thought can be opposed by another thought.

But the council was greatly agitated by the hatred it had developed for Christ, so it abandoned the path of religion and chose the path of irreligion.

The high priest asked, "Are you the Messiah, the Son of God?"

Then, Christ answered him. "I believe that whatever answer I give to this question, you would neither consider it to be the true one, nor would you like it because of your biased opinions. I also imagine that whatever answers I give to your questions, you will not like them because of my strong conviction. And, yet, since you feel you need my answers, I tell all of you that one day you will see the Son of Man sitting at the right side of the Almighty and coming on the clouds of heaven."

Listening to Lord Christ's answer, the high priest tore his clothes in anger, as if his religious heart were shattered by this blasphemy. Eventually, he sputtered, "This Jesus has uttered blasphemy in this council. Now, we don't need any more witnesses to prove his offense. This blasphemy you have just heard is the best confirmation of all his offenses. What is the opinion of the assembly?"

Impressed by the high priest's display of anger, they roared with indignation. "He is guilty and must die!"

Excitement was at a fever pitch. What more could be said?

Many spat in Christ's face; others beat him on his back; and many others slapped his face. "Prophesy for us, Messiah. Guess who hit you."

Basically, there are two types of speakers: one type inspires others toward good; the other type incites others toward evil. Inspirational speech enkindles the divine flame of faith, love, dedication, and service. It replaces restlessness with peace. Inflammatory speech on the other hand, gives birth to faithlessness, hatred, selfishness, and coercion. It replaces peace with restlessness. The high priest's behavior may have appeared to some to be religious, but it was not. He was the second type of speaker—one who usually pretends to be religious. That pretense can also be called religious hypocrisy, and it is used to arouse people to hatred and to lead them to commit evil deeds.

The conduct of religious people is called respectable or moral. Was the behavior which Christ's enemies exhibited toward him respectable or moral? People differ from one another in their religious beliefs. If a person holds a belief different from that of another, does he deserve to be condemned to death? If some addict jabbers while drugged, "I am God"; if a psychotic claims, "I am God"; if someone claims with religious fervor, "I am God"; it is not proper to become excited by these statements which are merely an individual's opinion. One may believe such statements to be an offense, but it is inappropriate to impose this belief on others.

At this point, someone may question why Christ had to suffer such contempt.

A great teacher who holds the respect of 100,000 people should have the capacity to tolerate the disrespect of at least 1,000 people. If he does not have this strength, his greatness cannot last long. There has never been an instance where a great person didn't have an opponent or wasn't ridiculed or criticized.

Here, there is one thing worth noting.

I imagine that approximately fifty years after Christ passed away, a miracle must have happened. Many may have spat at Lord Christ; many may have beaten him, whipped him, or slapped him in the face; many may have mocked him as the "King of the Jews"; many may have thrust the crown of thorns on his head; many may have forced him to carry his cross; many may have cruelly driven sharp nails into his hands and feet, and many may have mocked him in various other ways. In spite of it all, many of their descendents have worshipped Christ as the Son of God. It is possible that today, even after almost 2,000 years, the adversaries' descendents are still worshipping Christ as the Son of God.

In reply to the high priest Caiaphus' last question, Christ had said, "One day, you will see the Son of Man sitting at the right side of the Almighty and coming on the clouds of heaven."

Of course the poor high priest was not able to have such a realization, but later generations have been witnessing that divine torch-bearer sitting at the right side of the Almighty.

Chapter 7

Peter Denies Christ

The night was not yet over. Almost 2½ hours remained until sunrise. It grew bitterly cold, and many people huddled around bonfires here and there while they discussed Christ. Peter was sitting among some people at a bonfire warming himself when one of the high priest's servant girls approached him. When she first saw Peter in the faint light of the bonfire, she vaguely remembered having seen this strange man somewhere. She stood there for a moment in reflection. Suddenly, she remembered. "I have seen this man with Jesus the Galilean."

She addressed the group. "Do you know this strange man?" Peter's heart contracted with fear and beat rapidly. Christ's enemies would become excited if they knew that Peter was a close disciple of Christ. They might condemn him to the same ordeal Christ would soon suffer.

Those sitting near the bonfire replied, "No, none of us recognize him." "Do you know him?" "Who is he?"

"I have seen him somewhere with Jesus."

Feigning innocence, Peter laughingly denied the charge. "Sister, have you seen me with Jesus? When? I saw him for the first time in this place. I don't know him at all."

The maidservant was confused by his deceitful reply. "Please forgive me. I am mistaken. Possibly it was some other person with him who resembled you." Then, she walked away.

Peter decided that it was no longer safe to sit there. After a little while, he got up and slowly moved toward the door of the courtyard. The servant girl had not gone very far when she met another girl in the courtyard. She said, "Sister, when we saw Jesus, he was accompanied by some other men, one of whom has come here. He was sitting over there by the bonfire, but after I questioned him, he got up and is now creeping toward the gate. I think my guess is correct. Go take a look at his face."

The other girl walked quickly toward Peter to get a good look at him. She recognized him. Returning to the bonfire, she said, "I have also seen that man with Jesus. Both of us sisters were together at the time."

Immediately, the men sitting there followed Peter and asked him to halt. They inquired, "Tell us the truth. Were you with Jesus?"

Peter replied, "Brothers, what is the matter with you all? I am ready to swear in the name of truth. Why are you making such a fuss over a small thing? I don't know who Jesus is."

They made him swear in the name of truth. And Peter, without the slightest hesitation, swore an oath.

The men returned to the fire, but they were still suspicious. After returning, they recounted the incident to people who were at the other bonfires and who had heard only bits of the conversation from a distance. They all stood up and followed Peter who had traveled quite a distance from the courtyard.

Upon accosting him, they found that their suspicions were confirmed. They said, "You claim that you don't know Jesus, but your regional accent indicates not only that you know him, but that you must be his close companion."

Peter replied placatingly, "Dear brothers, really there is no need to be suspicious. I have sworn the most holy oath before you, and I am surprised that you are not satisfied. A sacred oath on the Lord's name is the highest oath one can make. It can never be transgressed. Do you consider me to be so depraved? Again, I tell you, I do not know who Jesus is."

Just then, a rooster crowed. Before that moment, Peter had denied Christ three times.

Assured that Peter's impressive speech was the truth, the men returned to their fires.

Peter went out a distance, collapsed, and wept bitterly.

Chapter 8

The Death of Judas

With downcast eyes, the embarrassed sun rose in the east.

The high priest, the scribes, the Pharisees, and the elders had gathered. Their verdict was firm and unanimous: Christ must be put to death. Then, they bound him in chains and led him off to Pilate.

Since the traitor of the guru, Judas Iscariot, had shaken hands with the elders, he got the opportunity to witness their utter contempt for his guru while concealing himself. He had never imagined that the situation would deteriorate to this extent. He had been convinced that Christ would fearlessly proclaim that he was the Messiah, the Son of God, before his enemies just as Judas believed Christ had admitted it elsewhere. Not only that, but Christ would, undoubtedly, prove his statement. The elders were just like other human beings; they were overly eager to accept the truth. People claimed that Christ had performed countless miracles. If it were true, then, he would surely perform some miracles in the assembly of the opponents.

Had Christ influenced people only by his pure character, the question of miracles would not have been raised. Christ, however, had given more emphasis to his divinity than to the purity of his character. He had praised his own capacity. In such a situation, how could the intellectuals possibly be influenced by his claim? Thus, the core issue of the discussion was not his pure character, but his claim to divinity. Judas respected the scribes, Pharisees, high priests, and elders as much as he respected Christ. When he observed the contempt and irreligious behavior of these supposedly religious people, however, he realized that he had made a serious mistake in handing Christ over to them. Even if the question of divinity had been put aside and the characters of the two opposing sides had been compared, the character of Christ was both superior and ideal. As a reward for this mean task, Judas had accepted thirty pieces of silver from the hypocritical proponents of "true religion." But it had not been for financial gain. He had seen it as merely a routine affair.

Judas experienced great mental anguish as a result of this painful event, and his dormant humanity was awakened. His former close relationship with the saint was not in vain, for he repented of his bad actions and cursed his useless life.

Judas decided that before taking any new steps, he should contemplate the situation deeply and remain patient. He would take the inevitable step toward repentance only after knowing what Pontious Pilate's decision in Christ's case would be.

He hurried to attend the governor's proceedings and concealed himself in a corner to avoid being recognized.

After arguing with the crowd, Pilate saw that it was useless to continue. In a gesture of helplessness, he washed his hands in front of the crowd and said, "In my opinion, Jesus is innocent. I cannot condemn him to death. Do whatever you wish with him."

The crowd, refusing to change their predetermined decision to crucify Christ, immediately began making preparations to execute their decision.

This decision delivered an intolerable blow to Judas' heart. He mused: "When this incident becomes known to my relatives and loved ones, fellow-devotees, and those who are close to me, all of them will develop utter disrespect for me. How can I let them see the sinful face of this betrayer?"

Upon deep reflection, he realized there was only one final solution: suicide. He decided that it was far better to cut short his life by committing suicide than to live a long life suffering this intolerable pain.

Since the crucifixion was scheduled for the afternoon, many adversaries drifted away after the trial. The high priest had invited the scribes, Pharisees, elders, and other respected citizens to dine at his villa. Those who accepted his invitation began to leave, still discussing the trial. Judas followed closely behind them.

At the high priest's villa, when everyone had leisurely taken his place at the table, Judas arrived and placed the bag of silver in front of them.

The high priest, immediately comprehending Judas' intentions, spoke in a stern, angry voice. "Why are you returning the silver? We have given it to you as a reward."

Judas replied, "Forgive me. I consider this a sin, not a reward."

All eyebrows were raised and all eyes became hard at this offense. One of the elders began to explain their philosophy in a persuasive voice. "You fool. Why do you delude yourself? The money you have received is neither a reward nor a sin. It is a symbol of merit. It will increase your wealth and your family's fame. Such honor is given only to a fortunate person, and you are a fortunate one."

"You have faith in your concepts, and I have faith in mine," Judas replied.

The chief priest picked up the bag of money and, expressing his contempt, threw it into Judas' lap. "What do we care about your concepts? That is your business."

Judas was silent. Now he knew hypocrisy inside and out. He walked out slowly, taking the bag of silver with him. Entering a nearby temple, he left the silver pieces there. He begged the Lord's forgiveness for his sin. He then found a secluded place, tied a rope to the branch of a tree, and hanged himself.

Within a few minutes, his spirit became free from his body and set forth on its long journey.

Chapter 9

Total Injustice

(Here we backtrack to examine more closely the scene of Christ's trial before Pontius Pilate.)

The doors of the courtroom opened at the appointed hour.

Throughout the city it was known that this was the day of Christ's trial. A crowd had gathered outside the court-room early and as soon as the doors opened, everyone entered swiftly.

Christ's opponents occupied the front row. That group included the high priest, scribes, Pharisees, the elders, and several other respected citizens. Those sympathizing with Jesus also occupied their appropriate places.

Pilate, the Roman governor, arrived punctually, took his seat, paused solemnly, and then began the proceedings.

After the preliminaries were over, Christ was brought in and led to the defendant's box. For a few moments, the Roman governor scrutinized him carefully from head to toe. Then he thought to himself, "This person who has established himself in the hearts of thousands can never be an offender. His personality, speech, and character are different from the average person."

Pilate's manner, however, concealed his opinion, and he spoke in an authoritative voice. "You have been charged with misleading the people. It is also said that you have advised people not to pay taxes to Caesar. Furthermore, you claim that you are the King of the Jews. Are you the King of the Jews?"

Christ replied, "The path on which I am leading society seems to me the path of truth. I experience myself sitting on the throne of the hearts of the Jewish people, and I experience them sitting on the throne of my heart. This is the reason why I have been called the King of the Jews. This is merely a bond of love. Regarding taxes, I have given this hint to people in what I feel is their best interest. To accept it or not is their choice. It is everyone's duty to give guidance to loved ones. In our daily transactions we can see that one person's intentions are not the same as every other person's. So, it is possible that others may not like my intentions. Similarly, I may not approve of others' intentions."

Then, the scribes, the Pharisees, the elders, and the chief priest, Caiaphus, began making various charges against Christ. But he stood without giving any reply. Governor Pilate was amazed at Jesus' self-control.

It was traditional during the Passover festival for the Roman governor to set free any one prisoner the crowd asked for. Among the prisoners, there was a very well-known criminal, Barabbas. Today, the crowd had made up its mind beforehand who would be set free.

Pilate asked them, "What decision have you made regarding my freeing of a prisoner? Tell me, who should I set free for you, Barabbas or Jesus, the Messiah?"

Pilate had deliberately referred to Christ as "the Messiah" because he was well aware that the authorities had handed Jesus over to him because they were jealous. Moreover, a short time after Pilate had entered the judgment hall, his wife sent him a message: "Beloved master, don't be led astray and punish that innocent man. In a dream last night I have suffered much on account of him."

Christ's enemies were very agitated by the possibility of Christ's being set free. They had persuaded the crowd beforehand to ask for the release of Barabbas, and now they began to incite the crowd to shout.

Governor Pilate disliked their behavior. Yet he asked them, "What is your desire?"

They all answered in one voice, "Set Barabbas free!"

"What, then, do I do with Jesus, called the Messiah?" The governor expressed his confusion.

"Crucify him!" They all answered in one voice again.

Pilate remained silent for a few moments. Then, he spoke solemnly, "I have heard very carefully your demand to crucify Jesus. However, I must ask you all what crime he has committed, so I can justify putting him to death."

His words did not influence the adversaries in the least. They continued shouting repeatedly, "He should be crucified! He is a hypocrite, a debaucher, a threat to society, and a great sinner."

The decorum of the judgment hall was being violated; the atmosphere was one of pandemonium. There was no justice in the people's opinion, and their hatred for Jesus was obvious.

The governor found himself helpless. He asked for a basin, and, washing his hands in front of the crowd, he expressed his final decision. "I do not give much importance to your accusations. In my opinion, this man is innocent. I cannot sentence him to death, and I will not be responsible for shedding the blood of an innocent man. Let his blood be on your heads."

In response to this, the leaders shouted: "Governor, we are convinced that Jesus is a great sinner and an irreligious person. If we and our descendents are sinning by spilling his blood, we will gladly accept the blame."

Now that the judgment had been passed into the people's hands, they freed Barabbas and demanded that the officials whip Jesus.

When such painful punishments are arranged for a criminal, one cannot fully comprehend the countless faults inherent in such punishments. However, when a person himself has to suffer such punishments, it appears inhuman and cruel.

When civilized people witness innocent saints and virtuous men suffering such cruelty, they tremble with fear. Their hearts experience intolerable pain, and they cry out in desperation. Streams of tears pour from their affectionate eyes. Universally, people experience both the happiness and the pain of saints and virtuous men, because they all share the same heart.

The bodies of saints and virtuous men may perish, but the influence of their pure lives continues forever. Their lives are an eternal source of truth, religion, character, austerity, and divine inspiration. By their exemplary lives, such souls preserve both human and divine qualities.

Time after time, Christ's body was lashed, but Christ was absorbed in communion with God. Yet, often he cried out in pain, and often tears born of intolerable pain poured from his eyes.

Many of his enemies remained on the scene just to make sure that punishment was being executed properly. Concentrating deeply on the entire scene, they carefully observed the effects of the whipping on Christ's mind and body. Christ's cries and tears of pain evoked their mirth. "If he were a true Son of God," they laughed loudly, "would he accept being beaten like this? Wouldn't he resist? People say that Jesus performs miracles. That is absolutely ridiculous. He does not perform miracles. He fools the people."

Still unsatisfied even with this torture, they prodded the soldiers. "This is the King of the Jews. You should welcome him with the entire army."

The soldiers laughed. They led Christ into the palace, and in a short time, the entire army battalion gathered.

One soldier stripped Christ of his clothes. Another soldier put a scarlet robe on him.

Someone said, "The king deserves a crown. Why don't you put a crown on him such as no king has ever worn?"

Everyone was perplexed. No one could find a solution to

Finally, someone, laughing gaily, offered a solution. "The administration of a state cannot proceed without a minister. Appoint me chief minister. Make a crown of thorny branches and place it on his head, and make sure that the thorns are very sharp. Weave it so that the points of the thorns are pointing downward and inward, and make it slightly too small for his head. We don't want it to move about and slip off easily. Plait it carefully so that it embraces his head. Such an opportunity comes only after many ages. Be careful not to miss a single detail of this task." Everyone laughed loudly.

They quickly wove the crown.

Many in the crowd were jubilant. "Excellent! Congratulations to the artist. So, let us begin the welcoming reception for the king."

One of them placed the crown of thorns tightly on Christ's head. Streams of blood poured from every spot where the thorns pricked his head. Handing him a reed, they exclaimed, "Long live the King of the Jews."

The first session of the drama was over; the second session now began.

The agitated soldiers spat in Christ's face.

Lord Christ never wiped their saliva from his immobile face which was an easy target for everyone to hit.

One of the soldiers grabbed the reed from Christ's hand and struck him with it. They all continued torturing him until they were satisfied. When they had finished their mockery, they removed the robe and put his own clothes back on him.

The details of Christ's torture spread throughout Jerusalem. Many were overjoyed, but those who loved Christ were deeply grieved. Crowds of people ran to the judgment hall to find out the truth.

After the "reception ceremony" for the King of the Jews was over, the proceedings for the "funeral ceremony" began.

The soldiers forced Christ, who was exhausted from the

whipping, to carry his cross. He was unable to walk a long distance while bearing the heavy cross which slipped from his shoulder repeatedly. He had to stop intermittently along the road. Even in this pitiable condition, he was continually whipped by the cruel soldiers and prodded to continue carrying his cross. Men and women who loved him were walking slowly, wailing bitterly. It was a heart-rending scene.

Lord Christ's heart was the heart of a saint. When he saw his loved ones crying bitterly, he forgot his critical situation and attempted to comfort them. "Beloved mothers, beloved sisters, do not cry for me; cry for your unfortunate children, for the days shall come when people will say, 'How lucky are women who never bore babies, who never nursed them.' Your families will say to the mountain, 'Fall on us, oh mountains. Please fall on us'; and to the hills, 'Hide us, for if such things are done when the wood is green, what will happen when it is dry?' "

Eventually, they came to Golgotha which was known as the "place of the skulls." Christ was offered wine mixed with gall, but after tasting it, he refused to drink.

Then Pilate's soldiers led Christ to a cross, asked him to raise his hands, and tied them very tightly to the cross. Similarly, his legs were tied to the cross, so that no one would miss a blow while whipping him.

Two criminals were also led out to be crucified with Christ. They were tied and then nailed to the crosses which were then erected.

Christ's cross was between them.

Gradually the crowd increased in number.

Many of Christ's enemies were standing very close to the site of the crucifixion. Among them were the high priest, Caiaphus; the scribes, the Pharisees, and the elders. Christ's loved ones were also there on both sides and in front of the cross.

The executioner began hammering a sharp iron nail into one of Christ's hands. Fountains of blood jetted out. Many women screamed and fell unconscious to the ground. Among them was Christ's mother, Mary. Observing this painful scene, those who loved Christ lowered their heads. Yet, they saw the same scene on the ground. Trembling with fear, their eyes rained tears of desperate agony and distress.

No sooner had the nail been hammered in than Christ descended into the depths of his heart. He began to pray.

It was not a new event for many of those who stood close-by. Soldiers witnessed the crucifixion without any emotion. For them, death was a very common event, as ordinary as any other.

In attendance covertly, many of Christ's close disciples stood watching with blanched faces.

Some in the crowd were happy. They closely observed the proceedings with acute interest as if it were a festival.

Then the soldiers hammered a nail into Christ's other hand. Again fountains of blood jetted out. The entire atmosphere was filled with the pathetic sounds of countless sobs.

If some were experiencing excruciating pain merely from observing this scene, what pain must the person suffering have experienced?

Some of the people were goading the criminals who hung on the crosses near Christ. Excited by their coaxing, one of the criminals hurled insults at Christ. "Jesus, aren't you the Messiah? If you are the Messiah, save yourself and us."

The other thief, however, rebuked the first thief saying, "Brother, we have only a few moments to live; why are you speaking like this? Don't you fear God? The Messiah protects virtuous people. This Jesus is, after all, only human. He has always performed good works; he has not committed any crime." Continuing in a choked voice the thief spoke. "Beloved Jesus Christ, I am overly grateful that the Lord has permitted me to end my life in your presence, for you are dear to God. I have only one prayer to offer you. When you return to your kingdom, kindly keep me under your protection." He then closed his eyes from which tears of love began to flow.

Christ comforted him with affection in his voice. "I promise you that today you will be with me in Paradise."

Many of Christ's enemies heard this conversation, but they were not moved by it. In order to create a different atmosphere, one of them said, "Oh Jesus, you have swaggered a lot among people. Why are you so cold with us? You have said that the temple which has been made by hands will be torn down and raised up in three days without hands. You are so capable; yet, even now, why aren't you able to protect yourself? If you are really the Son of God, come down from the cross."

The high priest, scribes, Pharisees, and elders also mocked him. "Jesus, we have heard that you have raised many dead people. If this is true, why don't you resist your own death? You are the King of the Jews. If you will come down from the cross, we will have total faith in you. Furthermore, if the deity you worship really loves you, if you are his son, why doesn't he save you? Your claim of being the Son of God is imaginary. We, in fact, do not believe that you can save yourself."

Many in the crowd continued to behave abominably. The arrows of their poisonous words had completely wounded Christ's heart.

Why were the people who loved Christ silent?

It is not that they didn't have tongues in their mouths. Neither was it because they didn't know the art of using sharp words. A terrible fire of anger was blazing in their hearts. However, they could see there was no use in exchanging abusive words, for they were also in a very helpless situation.

The crucifixion had begun in the afternoon, but not a single ray of sun was visible. The entire sky was covered with dark clouds; it was as if the day had turned into night. The whole country was enveloped in darkness. It appeared that all of nature was deep in sorrow.

The moment of death approached. The crowd was silent. Absolute silence pervaded the entire scene.

As before, Christ's loved ones could only observe in sorrow the second part of this drama. When a person is in a helpless situation, his body, senses, *prana**, *chitta***, and intellect are not able to take even one step toward freedom.

Christ's pain-racked body hung on the cross. Blood streamed from both his hands which were punctured with nails. The thorny crown created agony each time he moved his head. The stripes on his back which had been made by cruel whips constantly oozed blood; yet, Christ continually prayed to the Lord. Indeed, the appropriate time for prayer is during periods of extreme pain or happiness.

It is quite usual, in such painful situations, for a person to be vengeful toward the enemy. But Christ was a saint. Even during his last stages of death, when his consciousness surfaced after bathing in the sacred pool of his prayer to the Lord, there was no animosity in his mind. Christ opened his eyes. His compassionate glance fell first on his loved ones who were sobbing bitterly. His gaze, a nectar of love, showered upon them. He gazed at them for only a few moments, but the effects of this nectar would last for years to come.

Then Lord Christ's gaze fell on those who scorned him. In that moment he was everyone's benefactor. His mind was completely absorbed in praying to the Lord.

He spoke spontaneously. "Oh, compassionate Father, forgive them; they deserve to be forgiven, for they do not know what they are doing."

Only an extraordinarily great master could express kindness toward his enemies. Christ, indeed, was the Son of God, and he did not forget that fact even at the last moment

*prana — vital air; the vital force which pervades the universe
**chitta — "mindstuff"; the contemplative faculty of the composite mind

of his death. At that moment, he was able to practice what he had preached. This was indisputable confirmation that he was the Son of God.

Then the executioners placed one of his feet on top of the other and began to hammer nails through them. More blood flowed. Christ's head fell to one side. Tears flooded from the eyes of his loved ones. Their hearts were seared by the fire of pain. Even in such a painful situation, Christ's heart was manifesting tender melodies of his prayer to the Lord.

Evening approached.

Although engrossed in prayer, it was apparent to Christ that death was quickly approaching. Now, only a few moments remained.

Lord Christ lifted his tear-filled eyes skyward. His body was pathetically pale. His parched lips parted unconsciously. Suddenly, his silent prayer was verbalized.

He groaned loudly. "Oh, my beloved Lord, why have You abandoned me?"

Surely there was intolerable pain expressed in this sentence, but it was not the pain of death. It was the pain of love. It was a confession of a devotee to the Lord. It was devoid of concern with worldly matters.

His loved ones heard the words of this last prayer and were totally convinced that Lord Christ was indeed God's devotee. If he had been otherwise, he would not have been able to utter those words in such a critical situation.

His enemies also heard his words, but they were not touched by the feelings of devotion inherent in them. They misinterpreted the statement as being Lord Christ's confession of being totally helpless because his God did not help him in the least.

A soldier soaked a sponge in wine mixed with gall and offered it to Christ at the tip of a stick. "Here. Suck a little of this wine to wet your parched throat. This will enable you to speak loudly."

Upon hearing those words, many in the crowd roared

Indeed, this was vile mockery. Even a heartless person would hesitate to commit such an evil deed. But this was an animal disguised as a man who believed and made others believe he was religious. He had no knowledge of religion. This was not disrespect for a person; it was an utter violation of religion. It was a totally evil action.

Another man, in order to intensify the mocking, stopped the soldier. "Brother, it is no use. You won't get any results."

A third person pretended to argue. "Oh, don't give up. Wait. Let us see if Elijah is coming to save him. Why are you so impatient?"

At the time, Christ was absorbed within. None of the actions of those on the ground below him had attracted his attention. Once again, a pathetic prayer slipped out of his mouth. "Oh my beloved Lord, why have you abandoned me?"

He uttered the words with a groan. His voice became a mere croak in his parched throat. His loved ones were overwhelmed by his words. Those words have become immortal and have spread throughout the world.

Then a soldier pierced Christ's side with a spear. Streams of blood and water gushed out. His entire body was now covered with his scarlet blood which ran down and soaked the ground beneath the cross. Finally, Christ's *prana* became free from the bondage of his body and set forth on its pilgrimage to heaven.

The cruel hearts of his enemies were satisfied. The hearts of his loved ones were torn.

One of his beloved ones, while sobbing said, "The lamp of Jesus' life has been extinguished."

Another loved one consoled the other by wiping away his tears. "Why are you talking uselessly; he was not an ordinary oil or ghee lamp that can be extinguished. He was an extraordinary global lamp radiating with divine light. Night is approaching; he has merely set for a while. Tomorrow morning, his light will rise again in the East."

Swami Kripalvanandji

His Holiness Swami Shri Kripalvanandji, affectionately known as Bapuji, was one whose whole life was an expression of his burning desire for God-realization. He was born in 1913 to poor yet devout Brahmin parents in Gujurat, India. From an unusually early age he loved to spend time in worship and devotion and developed remarkable talents in the fields of literature and music. Still, he felt unfulfilled. His desire for union with God was so intense, and his attempts to reach it so frustrating, that by the age of 19 he had come close to suicide three times. It was as he determinedly planned his fourth attempt that he was saved and guided onto the highest path of yoga by the compassionate master who was to become his guru, Dadaji.

Dadaji's deep love won Bapuji's heart. When he witnessed Dadaji's miraculous yogic powers, his mind was won over too, and he was filled with renewed hope of satisfying his unquenchable desire for God-realization. At Dadaji's request, Bapuji moved into Dadaji's ashram and began the close personal training that was to change his life.

After eight months of teaching, Dadaji gave Bapuji special yogic initiation, first requiring him to spend 40 days in total seclusion and silence, fasting on water, meditating, and chanting mantra. These were hard disciplines for a youth of 19, but Dadaji's great love for Bapuji enabled him to succeed. When he received initiation, Dadaji told him: "My son, my blessing to you is that you will become the world's greatest yogacharya." This blessing indeed came true.

When Bapuji had been with his guru only 1¼ years, Dadaji mysteriously disappeared. Though he had many devoted disciples, none had been able to discover his true name, much less where he had come from or where he had gone. Bapuji was left to pursue his way alone in the world, supported by his guru's last promise that Bapuji would see him again when he had finally renounced all worldly desires. Nearly ten years later, Bapuji finally took initiation as a swami, a renunciate monk. He traveled throughout western India, teaching the scriptures and turning men's hearts toward God. In doing so, his natural gifts as a scholar, orator, musician, and poet flowered. Bapuji was so eloquent and inspiring that many of his listeners were moved to donate gifts of money, all of which he channeled towards the building of schools and temples for the further enlightenment of his countrymen.

After eight years spent in this manner, during which Bapuji meditated constantly on his guru and practiced his teachings devotedly, he and Dadaji reunited in a remarkable way. It was in 1952, during a pilgrimage, that Dadaji appeared to him with his true yogic body in the form of a beautiful youth. Without revealing his complete identity, Dadaji explained that he had taken on a normal human form for 1¾ years simply to be able to teach Bapuji personally. Two years later, Dadaji again appeared to Bapuji to encourage and guide him in his sadhana. It was at this time that Bapuji began his intense ten-hours-a-day practice of Kundalini meditation, a practice which he has maintained to his final days.

In 1955, Bapuji finally discovered his guru's complete historical identity during a visit to Kayavarohan, ancient India's great center of spiritual learning. Bapuji was taken into a temple where he was shown a large stone lingam, carved into which was the form of a young, seated yogi. In a flash of transcendental realization, he recognized it as his guru: Lord Lakulish (Bhagwan Brahmeshvar), 28th incarnation of Lord Shiva who had reincarnated in the 2nd century B.C. to restore Kayavarohan to its former glory and spiritual power.

Later, during meditation, Bapuji saw visions of Kayavarohan at the height of its flowering. He received a divine command to restore it yet again as a spiritual center, not only for India but for the whole world. Though a penniless swami, Bapuji bowed to divine will, and now Kayavarohan is rising again from the ashes like a phoenix and assuming a new and glorious future as an international center for spiritual enlightenment through the study of yoga, world scriptures, music, and many other related disciplines.

In addition to overseeing the restoration of Kayavarohan, Bapuji continued his brilliant work as a scholar and writer as well as his dedication to his most demanding sadhana. For twelve years he practiced total silence and for the ten years following he spoke only on rare, special occasions. The only exception to this extraordinary life was his arrival in the United States in 1977 where he was so struck by the openness of the aspiring seekers who greeted him that he delivered the series of lectures from which this discourse flows.

At the end of that first summer in America, Bapuji returned to seclusion and silence, residing at the ashram named for him by his close disciple Yogi Amrit Desai. He taught a few chosen disciples, wrote, continued his intense schedule of meditation, and once a week gave brief darshans for the hundreds who came to be in his presence. In September, 1981, Bapuji returned to India and, on December 29 of that year, left his body. For yoga masters such as Bapuji, this is known as *mahasamadhi*—his final merging into oneness with God. To honor Bapuji's memory and continue his work, a temple and ashram are being constructed at his burial site in Malav, Gujarat Province.

Books by and about Swami Kripalvanandji

Science of Meditation. Swami Kripalvanandji. Based on his personal experiences, a comprehensive and definitive work on all forms and stages of meditation.

Bapuji in America: Darshans at Kripalu Ashram. A commemorative collection of Swami Kripalvanandji's biography, teachings, and stories.

Light from Guru to Disciple. Rajarshi Muni. The inspiring and incredible account of Swami Kripalvanandji's life history, focusing on the discipleship and yogic training of this enlightened master.

Pilgrimage of Love, Books I and II. Swami Kripalvanandji. Presents Swami Kripalvanandji's discourses on the yamas and niyamas, the ethical basis of yoga. In *Book I* he teaches on principles of conduct such as non-stealing and non-violence. *Book II* addresses observances such as compassion, humility, and faith. Illustrated with amusing anecdotes, the discourses reveal the depth of Bapuji's insight into practicing yoga as a way of life.

Yoga Experiences. Rajarshi Muni. A fascinating account of the many unusual experiences encountered during Kundalini Shaktipat meditation, written by one of Swami Kripalvanandji's closest disciples.

For further information:

Kripalu Yoga Retreat
P.O. Box 120
Summit Station, PA 17979
(717) 754-3051

Kripalu Yoga Ashram
7 Walters Road
Sumneytown, PA 18084
(215) 234-4568